HEART PSALMS

HEART PSALMS

A Journey to Emotional Healing

JESSICA R. SHIREY

Meraki Press

Contents

Acknowledgments

This book was birthed on July 22, 2022, during an E5 Life Strategies inner-healing retreat at Light & Life Church in DuBois, Pennsylvania. As I sat reflecting on an art piece I made in the soaking room, Katie (Beard) Zeliger followed the Lord's prompting, and challenged me to cry out to God in a Psalm like David.

My first thought was, "yeah, sure – write a Psalm – like David.' Pfft. But later as I put pen to paper, my heart cried out to the Lord in my first Psalm.

It was truly effortless and done in a matter of minutes with my greatest obstacle being my illegible scribbles on the pages of my journal. As I burned the midnight oil, only one Heart Psalm spilled out, but I sensed from deep within that so many were bottled up and one day would form a collection that tells my story.

And so, I'll forever be thankful to Katie for so boldly challenging me, which unlocked this gift that was hidden deep within, unbeknownst to me. I'm especially thankful that she not only embraced the publication of Heart Psalms but also envisioned its devotional component, which we pray brings healing to you. It means so much and is such a blessing to me that the Lord chose Katie to help birth this gift and bring it full circle with "Heart Psalms: A Journey to Emotional Healing."

I'm also incredibly thankful for prayer ministers with E5 Life Strategies, who have been instrumental in my journey to emotional healing and complete freedom, and particularly, Oscar and Veronica Montiel, who encouraged me to go deeper and lean into Psalm writing beyond the summer retreat.

I'm thankful for my divine reunion with my former youth pastor, Brenda Libreatori, who now pastors The Vine Free Methodist Church in Clearfield, Pennsylvania. She has been such a blessing to me - a shoulder to cry on in moments of sorrow, and a trusted counselor and spiritual coach amidst life's chaos and confusion.

I'm thankful for my church family that the Lord has so intricately woven together, especially Becky Brown's women's bible study group, for believing in me and this book.

I'm deeply thankful to my aunt Brenda Shirey, who blessed me with a trip to experience Sight & Sound's truly worshipful production of David. It showed me why I feel so deeply connected with David, which allows me to express myself just as he did in the Psalms. The production also became the main inspiration for my book's cover.

Lastly, I'm thankful for my Lord and Savior Jesus Christ; for His unwavering love, for healing my battered heart, and for entrusting me with this book, to bring a source of healing to you.

Foreword

There is a scene in the Lion, the Witch, and the Wardrobe during battle, where a rhino charges at a white witch intending to take her out. But he is so fixated on this singular enemy that he misses a small gremlin. As he races toward the witch, this little gremlin steps into his path and cuts him down at the knees. The rhino tumbles and is stopped short of completing his mission.

As a pastor and prayer minister, I can attest to the subtle forms of attack that come against many men and women in the body of Christ. As many well-intending Christians pursue Christ and fight the obvious enemy of apostasy, there are little gremlins that seek to cut us down. The Bible calls these "little foxes." Little foxes sneak into the garden of your soul undetected and sneakily dig up good soil, and kill off fruit-bearing sources of life. These "little foxes" may appear in your life as simple and seemingly innocent sins such as little white lies, sugar-coated insults, hidden grudges, the lack of follow-through, or an extra slice of cake after dinner. But there is nothing innocent about these things. They are insidious and detrimental to our overall spiritual well-being.

There are often times in the midst of passion and pursuit of big God-sized dreams or slaying big giants, that we overlook the small things that could derail us. Such is the account of Jessica's journey. She chronicles her challenging pilgrimage of casting down idols and overcoming food addiction through the use of deeply personal, poetic psalms.

Jessica's passionate pursuit of holiness and breakthrough is what brought our paths together. As she moved forward to conquer the enemies of her life through intentional inner healing, she found freedom and the unique experience of Psalm writing in my Prophetic Art Room. As I sat, prayerfully watching over the participants, there was something unique in Jessica's heart that the Lord was uncapping. Jessica's soft and malleable heart made her a ripe candidate for God's perfecting, refining fire.

After I gave her a brief word of the Lord - a challenge I didn't know would one day bear the fruit of the book in your hands - I stepped back and allowed the Spirit to work. In all the time I have known Jessica, she has remained steadfast and yielded to the Lord's working hands in her life. And season after season, her faith is tested by fire and proves true as gold. The devotional you now hold is a gift of the Lord, first to Jessica, then to all of us that know her, and now, hopefully, to you.

As you step into her story and poetic approach to healing, you'll find an honest friend who has fought hard and now walks the path of freedom; you'll receive comfort in these psalms, finding a voice that prays the words you didn't know you needed; and you'll come to know a sister in Christ that gently beckons you to lay your burdens down, and to surrender your idols so that you too can enjoy a life of freedom.

Katie Zeliger
Assistant to the Pastor, Light and Life Church
Owner, Meraki Press

Introduction

I left my heart battered and my feelings bottled up for nearly four decades until my first E5 Life Strategies retreat in June 2020. As I walked what seemed like an endless hall to my personal ministry session, I was overwhelmed with dread and sheer horror. I knew it was the pathway to freedom, but it didn't feel that way. In that moment, it felt like the sentencing for every messed-up decision of my past. Although I was at an inner-healing retreat, I had no real plans to heal, only to escape with my brokenness still hidden.

While staring into a metal wastebasket filled with crumpled-up tissues, I realized God had other plans. In between sobs, I poured out a story I'd sworn to take to the grave. Bound by shame, I was unable to make eye contact with my ministers. I will never forget the moment I finally did. With tear-glossed eyes, I looked up and locked eyes with two women ministers who gleamed with love. There was no judgment, only love, and assurance that "Jesus still loves you." That is a memory I will cherish as dear to my heart for the rest of my life.

That was just the beginning. It was during my third retreat that I dug deeper than before. I got to the root of my issues and began to conquer things like inadequacy and rejection. But somehow while stuffing my face with cream-filled doughnuts, banana nut muffins, and the vast array of comfort foods given during breaks, I forgot about my struggle with food addiction. Not sure how that happened, but it did. Maybe it was for a reason, maybe I needed a much deeper inner healing to occur before I could face the roots of the food addiction.

What I initially saw as me being scatterbrained was actually a divine setup, though you wouldn't have known it if you'd seen me at the county fair. I went from vendor to vendor: that pile of hog fries, a pumpkin funnel cake that was surprisingly disappointing, and then a thickly-iced monkey bread - a delightful replacement for my disappointment - put my food problem on blast. It wasn't just a week-long fair food indulgence, but an all-day, everyday food addiction that held me hostage for 40 years. I realized then, yes, at the fair, that I didn't just overeat at the supper table or occasionally in between meals, I binged all the time, especially when I was emotionally triggered.

So, one night as I soaked in the presence of God, I cried out in desperation for His help, because another fad diet was surely not the answer. In a matter of days, I made a list of the sweet-and-salty gods I'd sought comfort from for decades and bid my farewell to embrace an even sweeter comforter, my Heavenly Father.

As I began this healing journey, I struggled to articulate to God my deepest, innermost desires of my heart, and so I put pen to paper pouring my heart out in this collection of Psalms. There were tearful moments, prayerful moments, and worshipful moments, but through it all, He brought me healing and ultimately victory.

As your journey begins, it's my hope you will let each psalm and accompanying scripture and song(s) minister to you, so God may heal your battered heart just like He did mine. It's important to let yourself feel what's bottled up inside, to let out your war cry, to let yourself feel the love of our Father and worship your way to victory. When the song fades each day, I encourage you to soak in the presence of God and let Him speak to you. Jot it down in the provided journal space.

So, as I close, and you turn the page, I invite you to use my Psalms as clay. Mold them to fit your circumstance and as a daily prayer over your life. Your struggle doesn't have to be with food addiction. It may be drugs, pornography, gambling, online shopping, social media, or that hand-held device you can't live without. Whatever it is, bring it to the Father. I promise you there is no better intimacy than intimacy shared with the Father, so let Him love you. He wants to speak His truth over you and break every chain.

Day 1: I Turn to You

Dear Precious Heavenly Father:

My voice, my heart cries out for You – more and more of You – and I know You will hear my cries.

On this day, I cry out – desperately – as a wayward child longing to feel the love and joy of her Heavenly Father.

Oh God, I am so sorry for having turned to sugary comforts over Your loving arms.

And so, I repent for my waywardness and vow – from the deepest place in my heart – to run, run to You.

From this day, I will run to You – straight to You – in my sorrow, in my heartache. You are my sweetest comfort.

Oh God, fill me, fill me to overflow with Your love, Your joy. I long for You and You alone to satisfy me.

In Jesus' satisfying name, Amen

Meditate & Listen

"Your God is gracious and kind and won't snub you—come back and He'll welcome you with open arms."
2 Chronicles. 30:9 MSG

Cory Asbury, *"Reckless Love"*

_____

_____

_____

_____

_____

_____

_____

_____

_____

_____

_____

_____

_____

_____

_____

Day 2: Sweet, Sweet Victory

Dear Precious Heavenly Father:

My voice, my heart praises You who is able to give me this sweet, sweet victory.

Oh God, You are good; You are strong; You are faithful, and so I shout out victory before one brick falls from this wall.

It has stood tall and been thickly fortified for forty years but will crumble at Your name.

On this day, I praise You and celebrate freedom from my emotions and painful insults that make up my past.

Deep calls out to deep, and so I cry out to You, Oh God, to heal this pain and heartache that's welled up inside of me.

I know you will and now I shout out: "He's set me free; He's set me free!

"May God be the Glory!"

In Jesus' victorious name, Amen

Meditate & Listen

"You will experience for yourselves the Truth, and the Truth will free you." John 8:32 MSG

Hillsong, *"Who You Say I Am"*

_____

_____

_____

_____

_____

_____

_____

_____

_____

_____

_____

_____

_____

_____

_____

Day 3: Sing to Victory

Dear Precious Heavenly Father:

Oh Mighty God of Angel armies, I thank You and I praise You – such a good friend of mine.

I have deserted You to lust after temporary satisfactions in sweet and salty gods.

Yet You have remained with me even after forty years, and never once entertained thoughts of departing from my side.

On this day, I know where my help comes from; it comes from the Lord.

And so, I cry out to You, Oh God, as fear and discouragement wage a full-fledged attack.

"Give me strength, Lord, and grow my faith – each day. Help me lay down pride and set my eyes upon You.

"Help me, help me give this battle to You – my One and Only true God, who hasn't lost yet."

Yesterday, I shouted out my victory and today I will sing praises for it.

In Jesus' victorious name, Amen

Meditate & Listen

"My grace is enough; it's all you need. My strength comes into its own in your weakness. Once I heard that, I was glad to let it happen. I quit focusing on the handicap and began appreciating the gift. It was a case of Christ's strength moving in on my weakness. Now I take limitations in stride, and with good cheer, these limitations that cut me down to size—abuse, accidents, opposition, bad breaks. I just let Christ take over! And so, the weaker I get, the stronger I become." 2 Corinthians 12:9-10 MSG

Casting Crowns, *"Praise You in this Storm"*
Elevation Worship, *"See A Victory"*

_____

_____

_____

_____

_____

_____

_____

_____

_____

_____

_____

Day 4: Sweet Like Honey

Dear Precious Heavenly Father:

My voice, my heart cries out to You, Oh God, to fill me with Your sweet and satisfying Word.

And so, at dawn's first light, wake me for a morning "snack" that I may nibble upon as I start my day.

I pray that Your "bite-size" words will renew my strength, and renew my encouragement.

As the hours pass, Oh God, prepare my "main dish" that I may feast upon when the chaos of life settles.

And satisfy my "sweet tooth" with reminders of how deep Your love is for me. May they taste sweet like honey on my lips.

Oh God, let Your Word come to me so that my fasting days become feasting days.

For I so desperately desire for You to be the joy of my heart and my sweetest delight.

For I know I have been called by Your Holy Name.

In Jesus' sweet, sweet name, Amen

Meditate & Listen

"You spoke to me, and I listened to every word. I belong to you, Lord God Almighty, and so Your words filled my heart with joy and happiness." Jeremiah 15:16 GNT

Andrew Ripp, *"Fill My Cup"*

_____

_____

_____

_____

_____

_____

_____

_____

_____

_____

_____

_____

_____

_____

_____

Day 5: Armor Up!

Dear Precious Heavenly Father:

Oh God, as my fasting days became feasting days, I place my mind, my thought-life in your hands.

For I know, the enemy hates me and will turn my mind into the battle-ground of a spiritual war.

So, remind me as I wake each morning to be still with my helmet of salvation resting in my hands.

Fill it – to the brim Oh God – with the cleansing and protective blood of Your Son, Jesus Christ.

As I put on my helmet each new day, may His blood cover me anew and fill my mind with truth.

Oh God, keep me in Your perfect peace, keep me steadfast in this spiritual battle.

I need You and Your full Armor to confidently shout: "Get behind me, Satan!"

In Jesus' mighty name, Amen

Meditate & Listen

"A final word: Be strong in the Lord and in His mighty power. Put on all of God's armor so that you will be able to stand firm against all strategies of the devil. For we are not fighting against flesh-and-blood enemies, but against evil rulers and authorities of the unseen world, against mighty powers in this dark world, and against evil spirits in the heavenly places. Therefore, put on every piece of God's armor so you will be able to resist the enemy in the time of evil. Then after the battle you will still be standing firm." Ephesians 6:10-13 NLT

Eva Mckinney, *"E6"*

_____

_____

_____

_____

_____

_____

_____

_____

_____

_____

_____

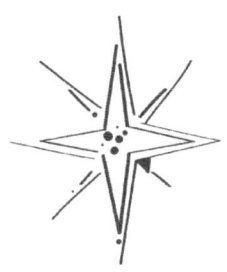

Day 6: Holy Hunger

Dear Precious Heavenly Father:

My voice, my heart cries out to You, Oh God, and I know You will hear my cries.

I must first repent for making Little Debbie my closest childhood friend.

Please forgive me, Oh God, for allowing her to lead my life-long worship of sweet and salty gods.

I also repent for longing and thirsting after sweet, chocolatey mochas and lattes topped with whipped cream and drizzle.

On this day, replace my "sweet tooth" for temporary satisfaction with a Holy hunger for You and Your Word.

Oh God, help me to long – so passionately long – to hunger and thirst after the only One who can truly satisfy me.

In Jesus' satisfying name, Amen

Meditate & Listen

"Listen, dear ones—get this straight; O Israel, don't take this lightly. Don't take up with strange gods, don't worship the popular gods. I'm God, your God, the very God who rescued you from doom in Egypt, then fed you all you could eat, filled your hungry stomachs." Psalms 81:8-10 MSG

Cody Carnes, *"Nothing Else"*

_____

_____

_____

_____

_____

_____

_____

_____

_____

_____

_____

_____

_____

_____

Day 7: My Crutch

Dear Precious Heavenly Father:

My voice, my heart cries out to You, Oh God, and I know You will hear these desperate cries.

On this day, I repent for allowing life to devour me like the roaring lion and seeking love from not-so-sweet confections.

It's left me so empty and even more broken, and so, Oh God, hear my S.O.S.

Help me! Help me to lean on You, and make You my crutch as the ultimate Good Shepherd.

For I know, You are the only One who loves me in the darkest valley and will faithfully carry me through.

And, Oh God, when I climb this mountain before me, I will surely know I didn't reach the peak on my own.

In Jesus' loving name, Amen

Meditate & Listen

"Trust God from the bottom of your heart; don't try to figure out everything on your own. Listen for God's voice in everything you do, everywhere you go; He's the one who will keep you on track. Don't assume that you know it all. Run to God! Run from evil! Your body will glow with health, your very bones will vibrate with life!" Proverbs 3:5-8 MSG

Will Reagan and United Pursuit, *"Nothing I Hold Onto"*

_____

_____

_____

_____

_____

_____

_____

_____

_____

_____

_____

_____

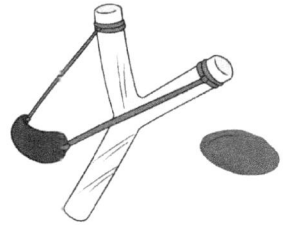

Day 8: Feasting on Salvation

Dear Precious Heavenly Father:

My voice, my heart cries out to You, Oh God, and I know You will hear my cries.

First, I must repent for fasting, and not feasting upon my gift of salvation.

And now, on this day, I say thank you, Father, thank you, Father, for sending Your glorious Son to save me.

Help me, Oh God, to keep my eyes upon You and the fulfillment of Christ's purpose.

Give me a Holy hunger so that the love Your Son has for the lost may transform my heart.

Fill my heart anew each day with the transformative love of Your Son. I want to pass it on.

In Jesus' life-changing name, Amen

Meditate & Listen

"Suppose one of you had a hundred sheep and lost one. Wouldn't you leave the ninety-nine in the wilderness and go after the lost one until you found it? When found, you can be sure you would put it across your shoulders, rejoicing, and when you got home call in your friends and neighbors, saying, 'Celebrate with me! I've found my lost sheep!'" Luke 15:4-6 MSG

Zach Williams, *"Heart of God"*

_____

_____

_____

_____

_____

_____

_____

_____

_____

_____

_____

_____

Day 9: His Presence, My Present

Dear Precious Heavenly Father:

My voice, my heart cries out to You, Oh God, and I know You will hear my cries.

First, I come with a repenting heart. I have been selfishly seeking worldly pleasures and treasures that are not of You.

On this day, I turn to You for I know, Oh God, that Your presence is a precious present from You to me.

And I long – so desperately long – for precious moments to slow down and sit at the feet of my Father.

As intimately written in song, I wanna "lay back against You and breathe, feel Your heartbeat."

I wanna feel this love that's so deep – more than I can stand – and melt – completely melt – in Your peace.

In Jesus' loving name, Amen

Meditate & Listen

"Then [with a deep longing] you will seek Me and require Me [as a vital necessity] and [you will] find Me when you search for Me with all your heart." Jeremiah 29:13 AMP

"I love those who love me; And those who seek Me early and diligently will find Me." Proverbs 8:17 AMP

"And those who know Your name [who have experienced Your precious mercy] will put their confident trust in You, For You, O Lord, have not abandoned those who seek You."
Psalms 9:10 AMP

Kari Jobe, *"The More I Seek You"*

_____

_____

_____

_____

_____

_____

_____

_____

_____

_____

Day 10: Shine!

Dear Light of the World:

I hear Your commission: "Shine! Shine! You are the Light of the World."

But my heart feels troubled, and at times, my light flickers, grows dim and even goes completely dark.

On this day, I enter Your glorious presence to plug into my light source.

I call unto You – Light of the World – to shine! Shine in me. Shine through me. Shine!

Fill the shadows of my soul with Your radiant light so I shine, Jesus, Shine! In Jesus' illuminating name, Amen

Meditate & Listen

"Once more Jesus addressed the crowd. He said, 'I am the Light of the world. He who follows Me will not walk in the darkness, but will have the Light of life.'" John 8:12 AMP

Graham Kendrick, *"Shine Jesus Shine"*

_____

_____

_____

_____

_____

_____

_____

_____

_____

_____

_____

_____

_____

_____

_____

_____

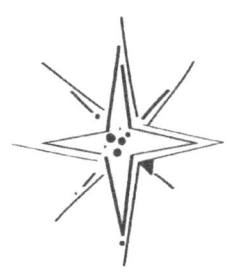

Day 11: Triggers

Dear Precious Heavenly Father:

My voice, my heart cries out to You, Oh God, and I know You will hear my cries.

Search me! Search my hungry heart as I stand before this open refrigerator door.

Why am I here? Why am I here, and not in your satisfying Word?

Please, please, show me these triggered thoughts that have me searching for something so unfulfilling.

Is it heartache? Stress? Loneliness? Show me, Oh God, so I may heal and so You may be all that I need.

In Jesus' satisfying name, Amen

Meditate & Listen

"Tremble [with anger or fear], and do not sin; Meditate in your heart upon your bed and be still [reflect on your sin and repent of your rebellion]." Psalms 4:4 AMP

"I considered my ways and turned my feet to [follow and obey] Your testimonies." Psalms 119:59 AMP

Bethel Music and Steffany Gretzinger, *"King of my Heart"*

_____

_____

_____

_____

_____

_____

_____

_____

_____

_____

_____

_____

_____

Day 12: Deep Calls Out to Deep

Dear Precious Heavenly Father:

My voice, my heart cries out to You, Oh God, and I know You will hear my cries.

You knew me even before You wove me so delicately together in my mother's womb.

For I know, You set me apart – even then – to reach the millions with a story much like my own.

But the lion came roaring with lies that I ate up while still a babe.

I was gnawed to pieces, and now, deep cries – so desperately it cries – out to deep.

Heal my most delicate parts and help me embrace Your love for me again!

In Jesus' loving name, Amen

Meditate & Listen

"For You formed my innermost parts; You knit me [together] in my mother's womb." Psalms 139:13 AMP

"Before I formed you in the womb, I knew you [and approved of you as My chosen instrument], and before you were born, I consecrated you [to Myself as My own]; I have appointed you as a prophet to the nations." Jeremiah 1:5 AMP

Ellie Holcomb, *"Wonderfully Made"*

_____

_____

_____

_____

_____

_____

_____

_____

_____

_____

_____

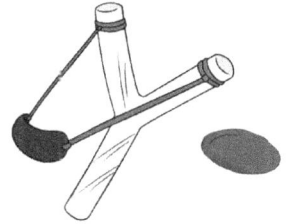

Day 13: Living Water

Dear Precious Heavenly Father:

My voice, my heart cries out to You, Oh God, and I know You will hear my cries.

I have been drinking from worldly cisterns that are broken and hold no water at all.

On this day, I thirst – so desperately thirst – for a cool drink from Your cup.

Cleanse my wounded heart, Oh God, and flood it with Your Living Water so that I may never thirst again.

In Jesus' life-giving name, Amen

Meditate & Listen

"Jesus replied, "Anyone who drinks this water will soon become thirsty again. But those who drink the water I give will never be thirsty again. It becomes a fresh, bubbling spring within them, giving them eternal life." John 4: 13-14 NLT

Olivia Lane, *"Woman at the Well"*

_____

_____

_____

_____

_____

_____

_____

_____

_____

_____

_____

_____

_____

_____

_____

_____

_____

Day 14: Promise Land

Dear Precious Heavenly Father:

You are such a good, good Father – loving me so incredibly recklessly.

And, even after You left the ninety-nine to find "the one," I ran. I ran from You.

You, Oh God, are the One true Comforter, Healer, and Savior, and I ran.

In my hurting, in my sorrow, I ran to false "Promise Lands" that were sweet and costly.

But now I turn and run straight to You – my one true "Promise Land."

In Jesus' comforting name, Amen

Meditate & Listen

"Then Jesus said, "Come to me, all of you who are weary and carry heavy burdens, and I will give you rest. Take My yoke upon you. Let Me teach you, because I am humble and gentle at heart, and you will find rest for your souls. For My yoke is easy to bear, and the burden I give you is light."
Matthew 11:28-30 NLT

TobyMac, *"Promised Land"*

_____

_____

_____

_____

_____

_____

_____

_____

_____

_____

_____

_____

_____

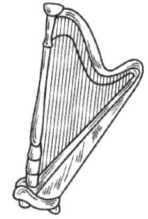

Day 15: Be Still & Know

Dear Precious Heavenly Father:

You are all-knowing, You are all-powerful and You are always present.

Yet, I never stop thinking, I never stop talking, and always am running from You.

And, in all my planning and all my talking, I miss Your voice, Your direction.

So, Oh God, silence my thoughts, silence my mouth. Help me to be still and give me a listening heart.

I really do long – desperately long – to hear more and more from You.

I commit myself to be still, to listen and trust You, Oh God, to do transformative work from the inside out.

In Jesus' caring name, Amen

Meditate & Listen

*"Be still and know (recognize, understand) that I am God. I will
be exalted among the nations! I will be exalted in the earth."*
Psalms 46:10 AMP

Community Music and The Church Will Sing, *"Make Room"*

_____

_____

_____

_____

_____

_____

_____

_____

_____

_____

_____

_____

_____

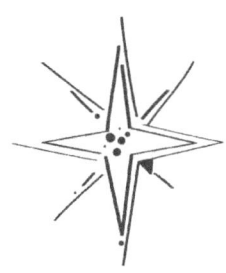

Day 16: Boulders

Dear Precious Heavenly Father:

My voice, my heart cries out to You, Oh God, and I know You will hear my cries.

I long – so desperately long - for more and more of You: Your attention, Your affection.

I Know Your love for me is so incredibly reckless, and that nothing can ever separate us.

But boulders have fallen upon my path, causing me to stumble blindly into the darkness.

So, I cry out to You, my all-powerful God, to blast these boulders that lie before me.

I hate that these boulders – big and small – are keeping me from experiencing the fullness of Your love.

In Jesus' all-powerful name, Amen

Meditate & Listen

"No power in the sky above or in the earth below—indeed, nothing in all creation will ever be able to separate us from the love of God that is revealed in Christ Jesus our Lord."
Romans 8:39 NLT

Crowder, *"How He Loves"*

_____

_____

_____

_____

_____

_____

_____

_____

_____

_____

_____

_____

_____

_____

_____

_____

_____

Day 17: Wake-up Call

Dear Precious Heavenly Father:

My voice, my heart cries out to You, Oh God, and I know You will hear my cries.

I am Your beloved daughter, I know, but have lost heart and gone through life so aimlessly.

I have been hungering for sweet and salty gods that send me into deep slumbers.

But on this day, I cry out so desperately for a wake-up call. Open my eyes! Open my heart!

Oh God, wake me! Rejuvenate me! I want to run the race You set before me with endurance and purpose.

I want to run this race at Your pace, and not grow weary, so heal my body and awaken my spirit.

In Jesus' rejuvenating name, Amen

Meditate & Listen

"But those who trust in the Lord will find new strength. They will soar high on wings like eagles. They will run and not grow weary. They will walk and not faint." Isaiah 40:31 NLT
See also, Hebrews 12:1-3 MSG

Kristene DiMarco, *"It Is Well (Through It All)"*

_____

_____

_____

_____

_____

_____

_____

_____

_____

_____

_____

_____

_____

_____

_____

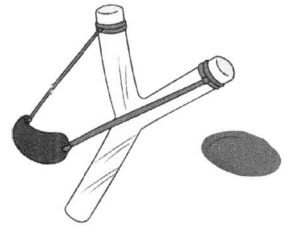

Day 18: Lamplight

Dear Precious Heavenly Father:

My voice, my heart cries out to You, Oh God, and I know You will hear my cries.

I have lost my way wandering down this foggy path into sheer darkness.

But I am not alone for You are with me, and by Your Words, I can see where I'm going.

So, Oh God, cast a beam of light upon this dark path. Be my lamplight and I'll never turn back.

In Jesus' illuminating name, Amen

Meditate & Listen

"By Your words I can see where I'm going; they throw a beam of light on my dark path. I've committed myself and I'll never turn back from living by Your righteous order. Everything's falling apart on me, God; put me together again with Your Word. Adorn me with Your finest sayings, God; teach me Your holy rules. My life is as close as my own hands, but I don't forget what You have revealed. The wicked do their best to throw me off track, but I don't swerve an inch from Your course. I inherited Your book on living; it's mine forever— what a gift! And how happy it makes me! I concentrate on doing exactly what You say— I always have and always will." Psalms 119:105-112 MSG

Michael W. Smith & Amy Grant, *"Thy Word"*

_____

_____

_____

_____

_____

_____

_____

_____

_____

Day 19: Hunger Pangs

Dear Precious Heavenly Father:

My heart, my soul clangs for You, Oh God, like Sunday morning church bells.

I've grown thirsty, I've grown hungry passing through this barren desert land.

Yes, Lord, I am hungry and Yes Lord, this journey You've chosen has me weary.

But don't dull this pain that clangs out from deep within me, intensify the pain. Yes, intensify!

Hear these clanging hunger pangs, Oh God, and use them to call me unto You.

In Jesus' intensifying name, Amen

Meditate & Listen

"God—You're my God! I can't get enough of You! I've worked up such hunger and thirst for God, traveling across dry and weary deserts." Psalms 63:1 MSG

"I lift my hands to You in prayer. I thirst for You as parched land thirsts for rain." Psalms 143:6 NLT

"Jesus said to them, "I am the bread of life; he who comes to Me will not hunger, and he who believes in Me will never thirst." John 6:35 NASB 1995

Jordan St. Cyr, *"Weary Traveler"*

_____

_____

_____

_____

_____

_____

_____

_____

_____

_____

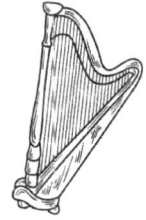

Day 20: A New Heart

Dear Precious Heavenly Father:

My voice, my heart cries out to You, Oh God, and I know You will hear my cries.

All of heaven rejoiced over my creation in the darkness of my mother's womb.

Your thoughts were so precious toward me as You knit me together so delicately.

My every moment was penned by You – my loving Father – before the dawn of my first day.

But life has left this heart battered and Your most delicate pieces scattered.

So, with Your healing hands, do another marvelous work; reknit this heart, Oh God, so it may beat again!

In Jesus' loving name, Amen

Meditate & Listen

"He will wipe every tear from their eyes, and there will be no more death or sorrow or crying or pain. All these things are gone forever." Revelation 21:4 NLT

"The Lord is close to the brokenhearted; He rescues those whose spirits are crushed." Psalms 34:18 NLT

"He heals the brokenhearted and bandages their wounds." Psalms 147:3 NLT

Matthew West, *"Broken Girl" and "Mended"*

_____

_____

_____

_____

_____

_____

_____

_____

_____

_____

_____

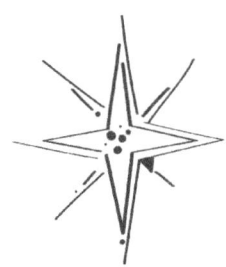

Day 21: Redeeming Love

Dear Precious Heavenly Father:

You are an all-knowing and ever-present God, who fusses over the intricate details of me.

Yet, my mind, and my heart races over this 1982 mystery novel You penned in heaven above.

Pages and chapters tell of my rejection, lost innocence, and heartbreak.

I've clung to this false identity far too long and yearned for the embrace of Your redeeming love.

So, kneeling humbly before Your holy throne, I lay this battered heart in the palm of Your hand.

Heal each layer – from the inside out – and may it testify to the heart of my Father.

In Jesus' redemptive name, Amen

Meditate & Listen

"I've wiped the slate of all your wrongdoings. There's nothing left of your sins. Come back to me, come back. I've redeemed you." Isaiah 44:22 MSG

"We have therefore been buried with Him through baptism into death, so that just as Christ was raised from the dead through the glory and power of the Father, we too might walk habitually in newness of life [abandoning our old ways]." Romans 6:4 AMP

Mercy Me, *"Flawless"*
Katy Nichole with Big Daddy Weave, *"God is in this Story"*

_____

_____

_____

_____

_____

_____

_____

_____

_____

_____

Day 22: "Feed My Sheep"

Dear Precious Heavenly Father:

I do love you- so deeply love you – with all my heart, all my soul, and all my mind.

I'm so sorrowful over this self-absorbed heart of mine that has neglected Your flock.

Oh God, You are love and I am not the only sheep whom You love and desire.

So, help me! Help me turn my inward gaze upon those who have fallen astray.

Perhaps it's the helpless lamb swallowed by rejection or the sheep captured by a wilderness of sin.

Guide our paths so they may cross and so I may fulfill Your command to: "Feed My Sheep."

In Jesus' satisfying name, Amen

Meditate & Listen

"He said to him the third time, "Simon, son of John, do you love Me [with a deep, personal affection for Me, as for a close friend]?" Peter was grieved that He asked him the third time, "Do you [really] love Me [with a deep, personal affection, as for a close friend]?" And he said to Him, "Lord, You know everything; You know that I love You [with a deep, personal affection, as for a close friend]." Jesus said to him, "Feed My sheep."
John 21:17 AMP

Cain, "The Commission"

_____

_____

_____

_____

_____

_____

_____

_____

_____

_____

_____

_____

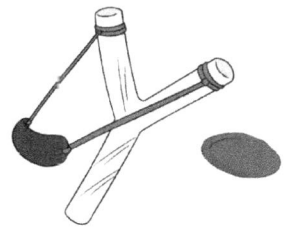

Day 23: Ditto & Amen

Dear Precious Heavenly Father:

My heart aches, my heart groans from the break of dawn to the midnight hour.

I sit here alone wearing a blank stare and begin to fall into this dark pit of despair.

My heart swells with a chord of emotions, stifling my ability to articulate this prayer.

But Your Son, Your Spirit, they hear my groaning, and I know they care – deeply care - for me.

So, I will rest in prayers they whispered for me into the Father's ear, and to that, I add my faith-filled "Ditto & Amen."

In Jesus' caring name, Amen

Meditate & Listen

"Meanwhile, the moment we get tired in the waiting, God's Spirit is right alongside helping us along. If we don't know how or what to pray, it doesn't matter. He does our praying in and for us, making prayer out of our wordless sighs, our aching groans. He knows us far better than we know ourselves, knows our pregnant condition, and keeps us present before God. That's why we can be so sure that every detail in our lives of love for God is worked into something good." Romans 8:26-27 MSG

Riley Clemmons, *"For the Good"*

_____

_____

_____

_____

_____

_____

_____

_____

_____

_____

_____

_____

Day 24: Banquet Table

Dear Precious Heavenly Father:

I stand here in awe of You. How marvelous, how wonderful You are!

What love You must have for me to give Your son up at Calvary.

What love Christ must have to die so we may partake in Your splendor together.

What love You must have, Oh God, for this intimate union that will endure forever.

What love Christ must have to set a place, especially for me at heaven's banquet table.

What love Christ must have that He would so desire to break bread and sup with me!

What love You must have that Your Son would invite me to "come to the table" today.

In Jesus' loving name, Amen

Meditate & Listen

"He brought me to the banqueting house, and his banner over me was love." Song of Solomon 2:4 ESV

"How happy are those servants whose Master finds them awake and ready when He returns! I tell you, He will take off His coat, have them sit down, and will wait on them." Luke 12:37 GNT

Sidewalk Prophets, *"Come to the Table"*

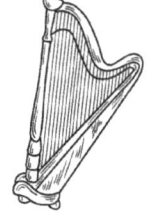

Day 25: Refining Fire

Dear Precious Heavenly Father:

My voice, my heart cries out to You, Oh God, and I know You will hear my cries.

I gently lay this complacent heart in Your hands for it cannot remain hidden any longer.

It's quieted my faith and roused fear, making me slothful - downright sleepy – here on these earthy laurels.

Wake me, wake me like the morning sun, and cast Your revelation light upon my innermost darkness.

Turn up Your "Holy Thermostat," heat up Your fiery furnace, Oh God, and I shall submit to Your refining fire.

Do a wondrous work, make this heart so beautiful, beautiful again.

In Jesus' refining name, Amen

Meditate & Listen

"And I will test the third that survives and will purify them as silver is purified by fire. I will test them as gold is tested. Then they will pray to Me, and I will answer them. I will tell them that they are My people, and they will confess that I am their God." Zechariah 13:9 GNT

"Gold and silver are tested by fire, and a person's heart is tested by the Lord." Proverbs 17:3 GNT

Jordan St. Cyr, *"Fires"*

_____

_____

_____

_____

_____

_____

_____

_____

_____

_____

_____

_____

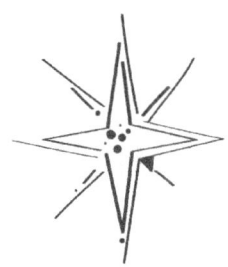

Day 26: Brick-by-Brick

Dear Precious Heavenly Father:

My voice, my heart cries out to You, Almighty God, and I know You will hear my cries.

Brick-by-brick, these foolish hands have torn down protective walls You so lovingly built.

And now, the prince of darkness has taken my identity, my destiny captive.

I love You – God and call unto You this day as my strong Protector to rescue me.

Yes! Snatch me from this relentless siege to the safety and security of Your castle's keep.

May it be our secret place where You may restore what's been lost and broken.

Rebuild Your protective walls, brick-by-brick, Oh God, and lovingly resurrect me.

In Jesus' resurrecting name, Amen

Meditate & Listen

"He who dwells in the shelter of the Most High Will remain secure and rest in the shadow of the Almighty [whose power no enemy can withstand]. I will say of the Lord, "He is my refuge and my fortress, My God, in whom I trust [with great confidence, and on whom I rely]!" For He will save you from the trap of the fowler, And from the deadly pestilence. He will cover you and completely protect you with His pinions, And under His wings you will find refuge; His faithfulness is a shield and a wall." Psalms 91:1-4 AMP

Lauren Daigle, *"Rescue"*

_____

_____

_____

_____

_____

_____

_____

_____

_____

_____

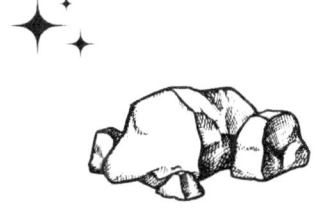

Day 27: Heavenly Promenade

Dear Precious Heavenly Father:

My voice, my heart cries out to You, Oh God, and I know You hear my cries. For I know, You're near, and not far off, for I know, You're always with me. I am Your beloved warrior daughter whose life tells a redemptive love story.

Lost I wandered down this messed-up path so desperate for "happily ever after."

You found me there – so cold and loveless - in the darkness of mourning.

Even still, You swept me away to dance this heavenly promenade.

But our love story has gone untold far too long; silence my fear, Oh God, and clothe me with boldness.

In Jesus' glorious name, Amen

Meditate & Listen

"But as for me, how wonderful to be near God, to find protection with the Sovereign Lord and to proclaim all that He has done!"
Psalms 73:28 GNT

Tasha Layton, *"Look What You've Done"*

_____

_____

_____

_____

_____

_____

_____

_____

_____

_____

_____

_____

_____

_____

_____

Day 28: Unlock My Heart

Dear Precious Heavenly Father:

You're an all-loving God whose heart desires to give me the Kingdom.

You withhold no good gift from me, yet the prayers of my heart remain such a mystery.

So, help me, Oh God, to unlock the innermost chambers of my heart to You.

For I long – so desperately long – to not just seek You but find You, my loving, giving Father!

My heart groans for more of You, to share an intimate dialogue without end.

In Jesus' loving name, Amen

Meditate & Listen

"Call to me, and I will answer you; I will tell you wonderful and marvelous things that you know nothing about."
Jeremiah 33:3 GNT

Lauren Daigle, *"Here's My Heart"*

_____

_____

_____

_____

_____

_____

_____

_____

_____

_____

_____

_____

_____

_____

_____

_____

Day 29: Streams

Dear Precious Heavenly Father:

You're my creative Creator who brings life and makes all things new.

My roots, however, are firmly planted beside a stream that flows of lies.

Downcast thoughts of inadequacy sprouted and self-hatred flourished.

So, dig deep, yes Lord, dig deep; get down to the roots and yank mightily!

Replant me beside the stream that brings life, that nourishes with Your truth.

In Jesus' nourishing name, Amen

Meditate & Listen

"Instead, you thrill to God's Word, you chew on Scripture day and night. You're a tree replanted in Eden, bearing fresh fruit every month, Never dropping a leaf, always in blossom."
Psalms 1:2–3 MSG

Riley Clemmons, *"Irreplaceable"*
Lauren Daigle, *"You Say"*

_____

_____

_____

_____

_____

_____

_____

_____

_____

_____

_____

_____

_____

_____

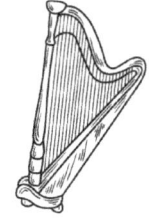

Day 30: Bondage-breaking Day

Dear Precious Heavenly Father:

It is for freedom that Christ has set us free, and You desire that for me.

Yet I have borne this harness of slavery that steers me away, so far away.

But today is my day – my bondage-breaking day – to boldly and firmly take a stand.

So, teach me! Teach me, Oh God, how to live freely and how to live well.

Satisfy me each morning with Your unfailing love that I may skip and sing for joy.

Oh, take these gloomy days and turn them into glory days spent reveling in You.

In Jesus' satisfying name, Amen

Meditate & Listen

"Christ has set us free to live a free life. So, take your stand!
Never again let anyone put a harness of slavery on you."
Galatians 5:1 MSG

"Celebrate God all day, every day. I mean, revel in him!"
Philippians 4:4 MSG

Katy Nichole, *"Jesus Changed My Life"*
Phil Wickham, *"House of the Lord"*

_____

_____

_____

_____

_____

_____

_____

_____

_____

_____

_____

_____

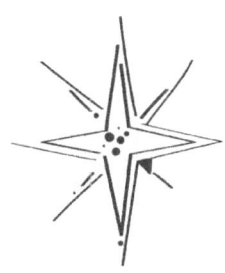

Reflection

_____
_____
_____
_____
_____
_____
_____
_____
_____
_____
_____
_____
_____
_____
_____
_____
_____
_____
_____
_____

Reflection

_____
_____
_____
_____
_____
_____
_____
_____
_____
_____
_____
_____
_____
_____
_____
_____
_____
_____
_____

Reflection

Reflection

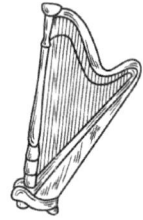

Reflection

_____
_____
_____
_____
_____
_____
_____
_____
_____
_____
_____
_____
_____
_____
_____
_____
_____
_____
_____

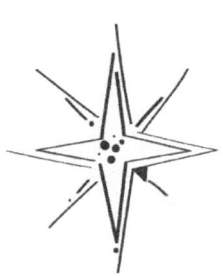

About Jessica

Jessica grew up in a Christian home nestled in the wooded hills of Shiloh, Pennsylvania.

The first-time author works as an online news editor with over 15 years of journalism experience. She also serves year-round as a media volunteer for Samaritan's Purse's Operation Christmas Child.

Currently, Jessica faithfully attends The Vine Free Methodist Church of Clearfield, Pennsylvania. She serves on the church's sound team, teaches junior church, and assists with its Operation Christmas Child Shoebox Project.

Jessica is represented by Katie Zeliger of Meraki Press.

Visit: https://heartpsalms22.wixsite.com/book

www.ingramcontent.com/pod-product-compliance
Lightning Source LLC
Chambersburg PA
CBHW060348130626
46553CB00003B/1140